THE GLASS

Sarah
with all good wishes
for your future career
& thanks for your work
for Literature

George Mary
Dec '94

Also by Gladys Mary Coles

Poetry

The Sounding Circle
Sinerva And Other Poems
The Snow Bird Sequence
Stoat, in Winter
Liverpool Folio
Studies in Stone
Leafburners: New and Selected Poems

Biography and Criticism

The Flower of Light: A Biography of Mary Webb
Introductions to Mary Webb's novels *Gone to Earth*
and *Precious Bane*
Introduction to Mary Webb's essays *The Spring of Joy*
Mary Webb: a new biography
Walks with Writers (with Gordon Dickins)

As Editor

Selected Poems of Mary Webb
Mary Webb: Collected Prose and Poems
Both Sides of the River: Merseyside in Poetry and Prose

THE GLASS ISLAND

GLADYS MARY COLES

Gladys Mary Coles

DUCKWORTH

First published in 1992 by

Gerald Duckworth & Co. Ltd.,
The Old Piano Factory,
48 Hoxton Square, London N1 6PB

© 1992 by Gladys Mary Coles
Reprinted 1994

A full CIP record for this book is available from the
British Library.

ISBN 0 7156 2453 9

Printed in Wales by:
GEE & SON LTD., DENBIGH, CLWYD

ACKNOWLEDGEMENTS

to the following journals and anthologies in which many of these poems first appeared:

Acumen, Borderlines, Critical Survey (Oxford University Press), *Cheshire Life, Environment Caring Poetry Festival 1991, Hepworth: A Celebration* (editor David Woolley, *Westwords*, 1992), *Lancaster Literature Festival 1987, Manchester Poets Open Competition Anthology, New Lines, New Welsh Review, Ore, Other Poetry, Outposts, Poetry from Aberystwyth VI, Poetry Wales, Staple, Transformation: the Poetry of Spiritual Consciousness* (editor Jay Ramsay, Rivelin-Grapheme, 1988), *The Turner Society News, Vision On, Ver Poets Voices, Westwords.*

Some of the poems have been broadcast on BBC Radio 4, BBC Wales, BBC Network North-West, BBC Radio Merseyside, BBC Radio Shropshire.

With thanks also to Dr. H. Stephen Green (Keeper of Archaeology, National Museum of Wales) for his helpful and encouraging comments on the poem 'Finds: Pontnewydd Cave'. This poem was first published as a 'Headland Poetry Live Poemcard'.

'The Dornier' won 1st Prize in the Aberystwyth (University of Wales) Open Poetry Competition, 1991

'Late August Fireworks, Llandudno Bay' won 1st Prize in the Outposts Poetry Competition 1992

'The Dornier' was selected for *The Forward Book of Poetry 1993 : the Best Poems of the Year* from the Forward Poetry Prizes (Forward Publishing 1992)

'Heron in the Alyn' was selected for *The Forward Book of Poetry 1994* (Forward Publishing 1993)

Other poems won major prizes in the Cardiff International Poetry Competition, Leek Arts Festival Poetry Competition, Ver Poets Open Poetry Competition, Lancaster Literature Festival Competition, Staple Open Poetry Competition.

for Lindsay and Kathryn

and

in memory of

Sarah Jones

of

Caernarfon

my great-grandmother

Contents

PART TWO : JOURNEYS

Part One

Finds

'Poetry is the plough of time'
— Osip Mandelstam

PONTNEWYDD CAVE, VALLEY OF THE ELWY

These trowels unlock the earth
deftly lift wedges like chocolate gateau
chink on clinker, cola cans
the flat tongues of flint.

Within the cave's cool dark, again
men and women cluster, crouch
over prehistoric fires, forage
for likely bones, appropriate stones.

Excited by a possibility, they chunter
sifting the soil tenderly, harvesting
fragments of something, someone —
the worn milk tooth of a child, born
a quarter of a million years before the Nazarene,
an adult's ground-down molar
bones of a bear's forearm
the flakes of tools, leaf-shaped spearheads.

Satisfied, they seal the sepulchre,
depart with their hunting equipment :
silence reclaims the hillside
where, high above the wooded valley,
limestone reflects sunlight, signals
to the tawny Elwy as it slides
seeking the once-carboniferous sea.

FFYNNON FAIR

"such another well as St. Winefred's"
— Gerard Manley Hopkins, 10 September, 1874

In denims, with packed rucksack and a map,
she walks the meadows, thinking of her losses —
childhood, vanished like woodsmoke,
first love, turned treacherous last May.
But today there will be finds.
Look ! here's the holy well where Hopkins came —
he prayed, drank the water, sketched
a conjectured canopy, five-pointed star
above the spring. She stands on its broken stones.
How slowly the bubbles soar to the surface,
solemnly processing in a constant stream
near clumps of floating weed with worlds of flies.
Cows rub their backs on the ruined chapel,
loosestrife flourishes by the chancel wall.

Outside, she turns a patch of soil —
hers is a private dig, to keep hope alive.
Light fading, she lifts a coin, holds it high :
coppery-green, smooth, it's almost blank,
yet here's the faint contour of a head —
he's facing right, his nose is aquiline.
Not the longed-for Roman, but early Hanoverian —
this coin, she says, would have seemed old
to Hopkins. For her, a token of future finds,
with a few white starburst flowers from the well.

QUARRY, LLANARMON-YN-IÂL

Tonight the ritual quiet returns,
dust settling with the birds,
moon layering white over white,
laying claim to the crater.
Again a temporary armistice
between man and mountain.

It's Spring, yet the trees around here
seem reluctant to green,
seem to know they'll soon bear
the plaster cast their young leaves wear
until they're shrunken and sear.

Complete, the evening exodus —
those limestone figures in homeward cars
shuttling along the Alyn valley.
Tomorrow they'll be back
arriving like children fresh to school,
faces ready to receive
the daily deathmask. By tea-break
they're ingrained, walking sculptures
who seize the mountain in their hands
shaking out, with the stone, their own years.

THE GWYNIAD

Cast up by last night's storm perhaps,
silver on Llyn Tegid's shingly shore —
one gwyniad, scaly jewel
from Ice Age deeps.
I look for others, for a shoal
caught swarming in the shallows
where they breed: this fish, the seldom-seen.
But there is only one, shining in sharp light,
like the bright harp floating on new waters
above the lost luxurious land. A warning?

Here and nowhere else the gwyniad lives,
too deep for beak or rod, ignoring lures —
this glacial survivor, never rising to the fly.
Gleaming fish from the innermost fathoms,
I know my own need for the dark centre,
to linger in secret recesses, resist exotic bait.
The gwyniad dies the moment it leaves the lake.

WET SPRING BANK HOLIDAY, DEE ESTUARY

Most of the view you have to imagine
when grey presents its variations —
the opposite coast ghosting back.
Absent first are the field shapes,
a green collage of hills,
precise definition of copse and farm,
the massed browns of Holywell;
next, Moel-y-Parc retracts its long antenna.
Under a gauze of rain, the outlined hills —
curvilinear, cut-off, cauled —
disappear in the drowned distance.

From both the estuary's shores
this same shroud separating
coasts, cliffs, the sprinkling of estates
whose lights at night are fallen galaxies —
all dissolve in the vanishing trick.

The metallic Dee divides
yet magnetises shore to shore.
Staring across from each side, eyes
watch like wildlife in undergrowth;
or binocularised, strain to reduce the miles,
capture circles of someone else's space.
Dunlin, redshank, gull, in flight
link coast to coast invisibly,
alight on unseen sand-banks.

Always there's this yearning to connect —
the views are never sufficient,
yet every fade-out seems somehow a death.

THE DORNIER

The moorland blazing and a bomber's moon
lit skies light as a June dawn,
the harvest stubble to a guilty flush.
I saw from the farmhouse the smoking plane
like a giant bat in a sideways dive,
fuel spewing from its underbelly.
I remember how one wing tipped our trees
tearing the screen of pines like lace,
flipping over, flimsy as my balsa models.
It shattered on the pasture, killing sheep,
ripping the fence where the shot fox hung.
Dad let me look next morning at the wreck —
it lay in two halves like a broken wasp,
nose nestled in the ground, blades
of the propellers bent . . .
I thought I saw them moving
in the wind.

If the Invader comes, the leaflet said,
*Do not give a German anything. Do not tell him
anything. Hide your food and bicycles.
Hide your maps . . .* But these Luftwaffe men
were dead. Their machine, a carcass
cordoned off. A museum dinosaur.
Don't go nearer. Do not touch.

Trophies, I took — a section of the tail
(our collie found it dangling in the hedge),
pieces of perspex like thin ice on the grass,
some swapped for shrapnel down at school
(how strangely it burned in a slow green flame).
Inscribed *September 1940, Nantglyn,*
the black-crossed relic now hangs on our wall.
My son lifts it down, asks questions
I can't answer.

16

Yesterday, turning the far meadow for new drains,
our blades hit three marrows, huge and hard,
stuffed with High Explosive — the Dornier's final gift.
Cordoned off, they're photographed, defused.
I take my son to see the empty crater,
the imprint of their shapes still in the soil —
shadows that turn up time.

TAKERS

The Cockle War, Dee Estuary

The tide pulls back, exposes the beds
of cockles, vulnerable in glossy mud.
Motorbikes advance, reverberate
like low-flying planes.
We hear these daily manoeuvres
of the cockle convoy; from the cliff
we see them out there, black gulls
scavenging. They fill the gullets
of sacks, packing carts their tractors tug.

Days, months,
mining the mud
they're strung-out pegs on a line.
Marauding, guarding their ground,
they ward off incomers, compete
for the cockle coinage,
those shells of lime with age-revealing rings :
two years, one, none —
too small to take, yet taken.

Calling, one to another, they forage
in families, sons snared in their fathers' trade.
While nearby, on a sea-walled lake,
the leisure lads in shiny wet-suits race
clinging to their stained-glass sails.

Today, a gritty wind,
the boat-yard chinking,
all verticals an instrument.
Still the cocklers smudge the horizon —
dark question marks. Their voices
flung, buffeted like kites.

Here, on the shore,
the tide's tossed jokes. We find
a bloated hand (sludge-filled glove),
drowned pale hair (meshed sack-string),
swollen bladders (sliced-bread bags),
split leggings splayed across the rocks.

This detritus reminds us of ourselves —
users and spenders all our days.
We collect the spent shells. Sand,
home to other creatures, falls
through our fingers.

ST. MELANGELL'S 'LAMBS'
(for Alice Thomas Ellis)

This end of the valley
belongs to Melangell —
time cannot erode her name;
the blades of grass are pilgrims
at her shrine, legions of daisies
and the brittle bell.
Blanketing silence here
where moving veils of rain
efface the snow,
where the Tanat flows
from its secret source.

We share this sleeting rain
with shrivelled snowdrops,
slate headstones, shy hares,
all momentary beneath mountains.
Under the sheltering yew we wonder
in what season did Melangell
save the hare.
Was it in Spring, when wild yellow
lit the meadows, the Prince of Powys
came, the hunted hare abandoning cover
faced his slavering hounds?
Or was it in Autumn
below the bronzed Berwyns,
the hare crashed through bracken
into that betraying meadow?

Melangell herself had fled
from the clasp of a Prince.
The hounds were stilled by her glance
as she held in her arms the hare
not even a Prince would dare to kill.

Melangell (Monacella), seventh century, patron saint of hares, known as
Melangell's 'Lambs'.

LATE AUGUST FIREWORKS, LLANDUDNO BAY

The tide hangs fire, on a ten o'clock turn;
crowds, in the blustery dark, anticipate
pink flares, cascading sputniks, a false dawn.

We huddle under awnings, watch night-cloud
as the first shower of stars explodes, fades out;
successive wonders rise and are devoured.

Above the Great Orme's flood-lit cliffs and woods
detonations splatter the Celtic west,
denote real firepower in troubled worlds.

Our minds meander when the magic palls:
though lasers colour the sky, write in light,
I see childhood's embers, collapsing fires.

My father sees war-searchlights cross, re-cross,
two bombers hit, in flames, their crews bale out —
falling through air four effigies which blaze.

My mother thinks of far galactic stars
named after gods; November gardens split
by bonfires; damp squibs and burnt-out cases.

The final burnished rain fans out, then dies:
we're faced with smoky darkness; all that's left
the jewelled pier, the black incoming waves.

HERON IN THE ALYN

I follow the river, heron-seeking
where weed and nettle reign,
caught in my sorrows
and my imagined sorrows.
Flies flick and rise, torment
slow cattle. Willows trail the water
and floating celandine; maybe also Ophelia
singing *'O, you must wear your rue
with a difference.'*

Seeking the heron
I make unexpected finds —
the sludge of a water-rat's lair,
sheep's wool a ragged veil on wire,
a tree-wound colonised by fungus —
and suddenly I see the secret bird !

Hidden in a tanglebend
grey visitant in fish-vigil,
alert in the afternoon heat.
Such startled lift-off
of great wings, crashing
through boughs, attaining sky.

I watch the slow pulse
of its flight, the laboured ease,
diminishing into distance
with its weight of unseen freight —
my sorrows, my imagined sorrows.

FROM A CLWYD HILLSIDE

Along these accessible heights the Sunday walkers
come, sharing the scenery — col, cwm and crown.
Mountains of the skyline are familiar as relatives:
we chant their given names — Tryfan, Cader Idris,
Snowdon — and those of our home hills
on which we track the path of Offa's Dyke —
Moel Famau, Moel Arthur, Moel-y-Parc —
another litany of labels.
A gloss on raw geology; Pre-Cambrian aeons,
shifting and settling of massive rock
in that unimaginable time before we came,
humans, with our need for names —
securities handed down through small centuries —
and our inventions which turn against us:
toxic rain, grass that kills, caesium,
genetic chaos in the flesh of sheep.

Light now inspects the folds of far hills;
shadows daub out the known shapes.
Up the cwm climb my daughters, laughing,
flushed, their long hair buoyant in the wind.
They come through the heather, calling
"We've seen a flying pheasant and two heron
heading for the Alyn." Today they're safe
in the nursery of names — and yet
how soon their world could be denuded,
stripped to molten ash and melting stone,
new nameless mountains moulded
beneath disinterested stars.

THE GLASS ISLAND (Ynys-witrin)
Glastonbury

1. The Legends

> A green lagoon; marshes, reed-mazed,
> and a long boat gliding like the swans,
> the quiet swans drawing their invisible chariot
> towards the otherworld, the glass island.
>
> And the long boat arriving nudges the grassy banks
> where the only sound is the whispered sound
> of voyagers from a time before, their circular call
> to those, water-crossing, who come ashore.
>
> Centuries of comings, season by season —
> the grail-seekers, the pilgrims
> leaving no trace on light and air.
>
> The white perpetuation of belief :
> a midwinter thorn blossoming
> each ice-time in the melt-meadows;
> a windfall of bones in a buried oak
> 'here lie Arthur and golden Guinevere'.
>
> Words and wood and water —
> water a reservoir of beginnings
> speaking of pre-beginnings.

2. The Well

> A liquid torc around the neck
> of a pilgrim, reflected, drinking
> from the chalice of earth.

3. The Tor

Rising above other domes of grass,
above Wearyall and Windmill,
the island of glass under an unreal geography
of clouds, shape-shifting, pulled apart.
Cloud-drift, constantly dispersing,
reassembling, like the seekers who come
season by turning season : they wind
a spiral way up vestigial paths
and fade one by one
imperceptibly as the wild geese
flying high at twilight.

Heat, marsh-light and the glass island
glistening behind the sun's incense.
What shines is neither grail nor chalice
but sharp-edged shards, a glazed bead,
a fragment of window, water in a glass.

PEACOCKS AT RUTHIN CASTLE

On my birthday I heard the peacocks call.
Across the castle lawns their slow yowls soared —
urgent, imploding
one persistent note.

We passed the grey clutch of dungeons
to earlier stones of a spread circle,
the peacocks' cries pursuing like sirens,
my daughters seeking their fallen feathers,
the iridescence of the males.

Again those cries entreating 'why?'
Birthday greetings, my daughters said.
I listened for some note of joy or hope —
something to confirm my hold on love,
the continuance of the unbroken circle,
my family generations still inside life's keep.

Still the peacocks called, and what I heard
was, over and over, 'Beware! . . . Beware!'

ANCIENT MONUMENT: ST. NON'S AT ST. DAVID'S
(after reading the Department of Environment pamphlet)

No clue to its date or function in the ruins:
no distinctive features survive.

Not orientated in Christian west-east,
not probably the remains of an earlier building.

No skeletons in the stone coffins,
not even the Blessed Non.

No certain connection with the early Christian pillar:
no one knows why this pillar-stone is propped here.

Not used for religion after the Reformation — first
non-chapel, then converted house, then leek-garden.

No pilgrimages now to the well
no longer used for curing non-sight.

No exact location of St. David's birthplace in the *Life* —
no proof of the story of his birth on this spot: how

Non, his mother, did not save herself from rape;
no sign of the stone imprinted by Non's fingers in birthpains ⌐

Non, perhaps not a woman at all, but the male saint Nonna.
No fee to visit St. Non's.

WATER POWER

Cures and curses
and counter-curses —
this well's water
accepted all wishes :

Send a baby to Gwen's womb.
Please untie my stammer.
Cure Alun's black hairy tongue.
Make Edward Hughes love me
and let a sore spread
in the middle of Nell Parry's face.

Dropped into depths —
medieval believings.
    Stick a pin
    in a cork :
    throw it in.
    Rub a rag on rheumatics :
    dip it in.
    Rub rheumatics on the rag :
    hang it high.
Trees near the well
festooned with shreds
of hopes.

Earlier still,
a Roman at Sulis Minerva
cast his lead tablet in :
May he who carried off Vilbia
from me, become as liquid as water.
Only the God could read the curse —
its backward flow.

I come today with my own petitions,
seeking the well on Llanelian hill :
Let all terrorists' bombs
explode in their faces.
Give rapists the rot.
Protect us from Poll's evil eye.
Please clear my writer's block.

The hills are green heaven,
the sky a blue halo,
I look for the well at Llanelian —
no fold in a field yields a sign,
only weeds crowd the meadow —
Llanelian's landlord has filled it in.

I leave with my ill-wishings,
well-wishings.

THE SHOCK

At Anglesey, one childhood holiday,
I feared to enter the mouth of a rose
opening its red cavern on the wallpaper
of a farm guest-house. Shy in the extreme,
I also feared to scream, nightmaring silently.
That week, off Bull Bay, I saw
the sleek seals' heads
bobbing like dark corks;
and I was told, at Red Wharf Sands,
of the murdered woman buried there —
her head was missing, perhaps anywhere
under the beach. I remembered
when I reached for my spade,
made no sand-castles, trod warily :
even the seashells were suspect
like the sand, no longer bland.
On the headland, every branch
held a snail under the leaves
and my Auntie's matchbox contained
an earwig. Back for the farmhouse meal
I refused to eat rabbit, rejected the pink pie.

Returning to the sooty sunlight of the city,
the evening sandstone warm and welcoming
in my Grandmother's backyard, I saw her dear bulk
bending over a bucket and, on coming closer,
the sleek wet bodies of kittens
bobbing like dark corks,
here and there a face floating,
the slit eyes, ears all innards,
mouths silently mewing —
the shock, in sunlight, seeing
my Grandmother drowning kittens.

Two Found Poems

1. ORAL HISTORY

from a Commonplace Book, 1813

Lord Malmesbury remembers
old Lord Arran who heard
his Grandfather say he had known
the famous Lady Desmond who —
at the advanced age of 130 —
was killed by a fall from a cherry tree.
He told him she had danced
with Richard the Third
and that he was by no means
the crooked deformed person
he is represented to us.
Richard died in 1485.
It is therefore very extraordinary
that this circumstance
should be transmitted
by Oral Tradition
through only
four persons.

Williams Wynn Papers, Clwyd Record Office

2. WELSH WHISKY

advertisement of the Frongoch Distillery (closed 1914)

Drives the skeleton from the feast
of painted landscapes
in the brain of man.
It is the mingled souls
of peat and barley
washed white within the waters
of the Tryweryn. Sunshine and shadow
in it, chasing over the billowy fields
the breath of June
the carol of the lark
the dew of night
the wealth of summer
the autumn's rich content
all golden with imprisoned light.

PORPHYRIA

She's a Cover Girl. An Italian beauty
on the front of a glossy magazine —
yet she's been around for two thousand years,
her skull full of dust, sealed in a sea-wall.

Now jets of water pour from her eyes —
she's cleansed, photographed, catalogued.
They call her Porphyria, take her gold rings,
the bracelets she's been guarding with her bones
since A.D. 79. Her skeleton speaks secrets
to scientists; the biographical bones reveal
no babies, but the elongated arms of a weaver,
hard-working, with perfect teeth, aquiline nose
and her left fibula fractured near the knee —
probably in a childhood fall.

Stripped of her gold, she's her own jewellery :
the pale chain of spine and torcs of ribs,
circlet of pelvis and casket-cranium holding
centuries, the stored sea-sounds of a shell.

What of her soul's secrets, lost
in lava? Troubles, leaving no imprint —
not even shadow-shapes in sand.
Or the love her eyes conveyed; caresses
with her supple weaver's fingers
of the giver of the rings. And her flesh —
the sun of twenty summers on her arms,
salt of the dark blue Tyrrhenian Sea,
oil of the olive and oleander blossom.
But the flesh's truth and the bone's truth
are not the same. Our minds can search
for hers : the bones won't tell.

'LES ESCLAVES' BY MICHELANGELO

Imprisoned by the heat of summer Paris,
seeking marble coolness,
I find in the confines of the Louvre
a chilling sight — two slaves in stone
as white as ice.

In ropes not robes,
this one dying perhaps, or slumbering;
that one straining at his thongs.
Both bound more by stone
than by their bonds.
Once carved to be fixed
forever on a dead Pope's tomb,
these two from the marble womb
were released by sculpting hands,
manipulated into muscle, sinew, bone,
endowed with the beauty of free form.
Their bodies imply supple movement,
transcend still life.

The slave who slumbers, frowns :
his expression says
'neither is there freedom in dreams'.
While I, in my prison of hot flesh,
liberated by their white shapes,
always will be captive
to this sculptor's art,
these slaves.

THINKING HANDS

(to Barbara Hepworth, 1903-75)

No art is required
in cutting a turnip,
scooping out crude holes
suggestive of eye sockets
where the light of the mind
might shine. One keen blade
is enough, and a strong wrist,
to twist out the centre,
create interior space
where a candle might be lit.

As I look at my turnip lantern
in the flicker of flames,
I think of the small woman
who shaped stone to her vision,
carved ancient African wood.
She gave definition to the elements,
fused sea and space, solidity and light —

knew, finally
the irony of fire.

SON ET LUMIÈRE AT THE TATE

Heading for the Pre-Raphaelites, I stop —
hearing the words *paint's spiritual language* —
and follow the speaker, a guide with golden hair.
Like airy balls, more words — *light, movement* —
float, fall into my consciousness. Turner, at Petworth,
she says, shook off his inhibitions,
made water-colour notes for future poems
in paint. *The play of opposites he understood.*
I tag onto the captive group
carried along by her luminous flow,
the verbal penetration of her art —
interpreting genius. Turner, abroad,
his journeys of search and sight
unfold as she illuminates each work :
her bright hair vibrates, she strides
the parquet floor, points to a core of light.
Colour is orchestrated here. And here . . .
Venetian waterlight . . . The necessary balance of brown
Above all, the vortex, worked for, achieved.
Caught in the whirlpool of her words
like his fisherman's boat in a coil of sea,
or transposed to the high Vatican
looking down on a circlet of Rome,
the terrestrial's made translucent, I'm transfixed,
addicted, thirst for more. She ends.
Polite thanks. We disperse.

Arriving at the Pre-Raphaelites, I gaze
lost for words.

AT BASINGWERK ABBEY, IN WINTER

St. Thomas' night. I tread the meadows — cold
white grass underfoot; sheep, ochre in the fold.
I walk alone among the abbey stones,
the broken cloisters, rosaries of bones.

Is that shadow or monk in the transept?
Does a hand move the worn, studded door?
Whispered vespers or night breeze?
Footsteps or mouse on the altar floor?

I hear madrigals in the rag-leaved trees,
wind wraps around the ruins —
through the bark-boned building, there
winding up the winding stair.

Where white-gowned monks no longer are
their orisons at break of star
rustle now among dry thistles.

St. Thomas' Day, 21 December. The longest night when ghosts in a
locality are said to gather to elect a new king for the coming year.

WATER IMAGE

Raindrops slip from the lime trees
laburnum chandeliers are citrus-wet
the last shrinking blossom on the hawthorn
drowns in resignation to forget
and the new golden rose is liquid yet.

Part Two

Journeys

'But then begins the journey in my head,
To work my mind, when body's work's expired'

— Shakespeare, Sonnet XXVII

EAST LANCASHIRE ROAD, A580

Straight as a Roman road from A to B
through flat-pack fields, brown-wrapped or greyish green
a hinterland of the humming city,

this tape of tarmac stretches thirty miles.
Driving my metal cell, thoughts start and stop,
link to feelings, surge, seize up like brakes.

The winter sky is blank, an empty screen;
faceless factories line the road like crates.
I'm moving through, controlled by red or green.

Some fields surprise with sections of sad crops
dulled by the diesel air. I think of vines
dark yet luxuriant on Alpine slopes

where summer's bright as light on glaciers
and — lovers then — we saw the high garden
set in hot rock at freezing altitudes.

Here black ice lacquers the unbending road —
I've gone through lights, but were they green or red?
Perhaps I've crashed : now dead, driving forward

in my afterlife — this unending road.
From factories, fields, sky, no living sign —
only the traffic's physical demand.

CHARLES LAMB AT OXFORD

(for Colin Haycraft)

Spindle-legged, in black, to the Bodleian,
inhaling learning, he enacts the student —
for two days. Votary of the quill, the desk,
yet chained to clerkship and his sister
(the strait waistcoat always near to hand).
Denied 'the sweet food of academic institutions',
his visit is just a taste and 'long put off'
he tells his friends. To Lloyd : 'much gratifyed';
to Coleridge : 'a fine bust of Bishop Taylor at All Souls' . . .
but confides 'there is something of dishonesty in any pleasures
I take without *her*. She never goes anywhere.'

After the foliage of books, Christ Church's trees,
Magdalen's groves, the quadrangle of Queen's,
he struts, playing at Gentleman Commoner or Doctor,
imagines courtesies — the Porter's deferential nod,
the Verger's bow, a curtsey from the bed-maker,
and yes, the chapel-bell ringing for *him*.

Plain Elia forgotten, he peeps into the butteries,
cordial kitchens; visions the crackling succulent
(colour of ripe pomegranate) on roast-pig;
sees spits which might have cooked for Chaucer,
long tables, glinting cutlery laid in rows . . .
and Mary, the red knife dripping in her hand,
his mother a carcass sliced to the heart,
his father, forehead ripped open by a fork,
Aunt Hetty lying senseless on the ground . . .
sees, too, the salted meat Mary had bought
and which he, later, forced himself to eat.

AUGUST BANK HOLIDAY, CHESTER

The last snatch of summer hatches out
the crowds, late season flies, into the air.
They flit and dart in cars, drawn to cafés,
toilets, parks and the jampot
of the river-banks, attracted to the Dee
going by indifferently on its tide.

Under smothering brass sounds from the Band
they disgorge into boats, choosing
the pleasure cruise on *Lady Diana*
or cosy motor craft which gently throb
or rowing boats requiring rhythmic effort
wobbling when wakes unzip the waves.

In this interplay of colour, movement,
like brief bright blossom on the water
they share that floating moment in their lives :
all pass under the Suspension Bridge,
avoid the organised turmoils of the weir.

The day dwindles into darkness and detritus,
the Dee drawing on to its own conclusions.

NIGHT DRIVE OVER SHAP

The road twists upward, a giant's rope
on the bulk to Shap. I'd left it late
(low February light fades at five)
lingering over lemon tea at Windermere.
Trying to unravel my reasons for travelling
I headed for Haweswater
hidden in its long volcanic fissure.

Headlights questioning each bend,
beams indenting the dark,
I was strung up to brake —
on the right broken boulders
on the left a black gap —
I saw new meaning in the saying
Turn off at Shap and step off the world.

Frosted rain bombarded the car,
sheep were bollards with cats-eyes shine,
abandoned lorries littered the corries.
I pulled in to rest the straining engine;
ahead, like pale fish in a dark pool,
the whited-out hills slid behind cloud.
Reassuring to recollect the onrolling
over this road of northbound travellers —
almost I could hear the creak of carts,
carriages, the tramp of armies,
Bonnie Prince Charlie's marching south, limping back.

I'd promised to arrive by eight, not to be late.
Petrol gauge trembling on empty
I made the downhill drop to Bampton
pitched past the Abbey ruins,
down further to drowned Mardale,
shadows of church, cottages, the Dun Bull Inn
eddying in the dead lake licking
the ankles of the fells.

At last the Hotel, like a large stage-prop.
I swayed into the light, the warmth,
seeing, across my reflection in plate-glass,
endless fanged dry-stone walls.
The Receptionist checked my booking's date —
'You're early for breakfast at eight'.

THE LIFE OF A RUSSIAN EMIGRÉ
(Vladimir Zaaloff, Maître d'Armes)

He thought he understood the Revolution
even though — tutor to the Tsar's court
in three weapons — no one believed him
or listened, least of all his Bolshevik captors.
All too clear those last days in Petrograd —
the confusion and the shouting, gunshots,
crowds storming the Schlüsselburg.
He'd known in early September — the air rife
with rumour, the radical end of summer
approaching, scuffed leaves in Uritzky Square —
the Revolution was irreversible,
'Peace, Land, Bread' the cry everywhere.

No aristocrat himself (from a village in Georgia
where his father withered on towards a hundred, watched
by his mother, careful of bad meat, icons, wolves)
he thought he understood the Revolution,
witnessed the assassination of Rasputin.
But carrying no party card he was arrested,
swords an anachronism before the Red Guards' guns.

That escape through the high, slit window, a fall
of twenty feet, he'd only just managed, running
in darkness along the Moyka. Hidden a month
by cousin Nadya — 'Skoro! Skoro!' she whispered
as he left, sliding at night across the flatlands.
Finland at dawn. A boat to Aberdeen. The drift south
to exile in London. A language to be learnt
while the old language of steel gave him a living.

Familiar music, this clash of foils, épees,
the crueller sound of sabres. Physical chess
in Balham; tuned muscles; the generations.
Not to anyone did he speak of the Revolution —
not even to Lydia, his wife for a while, singer
in 'The Balalaika' when he danced, black eyes blazing,
A robot bomb in the next War claimed
the framed photographs — Nadya, her son Grigori,
his father at a hundred. Layers of winters since,
yet old wounds beneath the snow, ready to flame
like Siberian flowers.

POPPY

Embezzler poppy,
absolute in theatrical dazzlement,
pinning the eye.
August hedges gain red
of an Eastern horizon,
a Geisha butterfly.

Dissembling petal splash,
conjuring narcotic dreams
yet innocent of opium's power.
Symbolising death,
blood on grey mud;
neat in a wreath,
jarring the drowsing mind
to memory.

Blatant pronouncer of the exotic —
eastern correlative.
Frail deceiver, scarlet lipped
pigment rips consciousness,
tips the edge of sleep —
essence dually beckoning
to centuries of repose
or flower-span release
from pain.

FIRST TASTE

In their brass bed, caged
like lions, prostrate in fever heat,
Father and Mother were deep in Spanish 'flu.
I pushed my toy engine, fearing their groans
yet wanting nearness in the darkened room.
Fluff became steam in the funnels of my train,
boots and shoes lined-up were hills or towns.

Outside, discordant cheers for the Parade —
soldiers returning, the remains of platoons.
Our flag at the window was a rain-sodden rag,
red running over blue and into white.
I watched the marching khaki men,
their sudden halt at the Sergeant's shriek.
Like performing puppets they jerked,
stayed still, jumped to life again
as the gutterals pricked their brains.
So this, I thought, is 'War' — the word I'd heard
over and over, with other words,
'Missing', 'Somme', 'Dead'.

From the street, a shrill cry — *Oranges . . .*
Spanish oranges! Piled high, a cart
bright with fruits I'd never seen.
Father fumbled for a sixpence —
Sweet oranges! — it bought us three.
I felt the firm, smooth skin,
brought them to him with the knife :
he cut and offered me a half.
The centre was of blood — it overflowed,
ran down my hand.

WAR STORY

Afternoon heat invading the factory, she felt trapped
in her turban, tied to the insatiable machine
feeding it identical parts at identical intervals.
Sun hazed the dungeon air, as in St. Xavier's Church
with its soporific sermons she'd ceased to attend.
He would be writing from Ceylon, he'd promised.
Perhaps the letter was waiting at home
on thin foreign paper smelling of lemons.
Her mother would have propped it by the mirror
she always looked in, hating her turban-flattened hair,
the squashed sausage of curls. Yes, the letter
would be there. And she would read it, over
and over, like the novels of Pearl S. Buck.

The machine churned on, cogs clicking, clacking
munitions' rough music. The afternoon shift
was dull since he'd gone. The canteen . . . there
she'd seen him first . . . tall, smoking a Senior Service.
He'd smiled, suggested the pictures . . .
Linking, he'd explained, 'I'm A1, but exempt
as an engineer. Enjoy swimming . . . sometimes cycle to Wales'.
The machine seized the rifle butts in eager jaws —
she wiped the sweat sliding down her arms.

Gone three months now. The ring he gave her, twined
and with a pearl, promised all . . . 'I'll write.
Won't be long to wait. Hitler's almost done for.'
Her screams rose above the roar
as the machine consumed her sleeve, pulling her arm
into its rotating teeth. Fastened by flesh, she fell
when the Foreman pressed the pedal of release.
'First Aid!' 'Ring for an ambulance!'
She heard their voices from a far-off reef
like wavelets around the island of Ceylon.

The pain held all her body by the arm.
'Perhaps she'd heard — it's going round —
about her Bill. Married to a woman back in Wales.
We kept it from her as he'd gone to Ceylon,
but news flies . . .'
A bomb burst in her brain. Somewhere a plane
exploded in the sun.

'THE COW IS A MAMAL'

from the essay of a ten year old East London evacuee,
broadcast on the Nine O'Clock News, 29 October 1939

The cow is a mamal.
It has six sides —
right, left, an upper and below.
At the back it has a tail
on which hangs a brush —
with this it sends the flies away
so they don't fall into the milk.
The head is for the purpose
of growing horns
and so that the mouth
can be somewhere.
The horns are to butt with,
the mouth is to moo with.

Under the cow hangs the milk.
It is arranged for milking.
When the people milk,
the milk comes —
there is never an end to the supply.
How the cow does it
I have not yet realised —
but it makes more and more.
The cow has a fine sense of smell —
one can smell it far away.
This is the reason
for the fresh air in the country.

The man cow is called an ox.
It is not a mamal.
The cow does not eat much
but what it eats it eats twice
so that it gets enough.
When it is hungry it moos
and when it says nothing
it's because all its inside
is full up with grass.

N44, FRANCE: HOLIDAY ROUTE

Maize, wheat, vines border the road,
a straight road, one hour to Rheims,
this the country of Champagne.
The celebration wine from sad flatlands;
white of the white grape
from a blood-soaked earth.
Signposts are to cemeteries,
graves, as neat and thickly planted
as the rows of vines. No bubbles here,
no sparkle. On one side a crucifix;
on the other, a stone hand holding
a stone flame. A little stone for every man.
War is soil-deep here, though the maize
grows fine ears, the vines have luscious grapes —
all this ground seems tender,
vulnerable. Hardly breathing, not believing
in any harvest, least of all its own.

Yes, there are poppies, still in abundance;
neither are the larks absent, nor their singing.
Yet the peace now lying over this landscape
seems merely a transfer about to be peeled back
to reveal the real scene: battle, ambush.
Trees seem about to explode;
fields, copses, grassy knolls
all units in the strategy, the campaign.

While Mephistopheles drinks champagne
an angel smiles through centuries of war
over the cathedral door
at Rheims, where hotels offer the best of wine
and tourists stay, less to mourn than dine.

'NO FATHER, NO MOTHER, NO WORK'

(note by a woman who committed suicide, recorded by
Virginia Woolf in an early journal, 1903)

No father, no mother, no work —
the words which Virginia Woolf
could not get out of her head
after she read of the drowned woman
dragged onto the shore of the Serpentine,
this note pinned to her dress;
No father, no mother, no work —
words which reverberate now
as I read of a woman
drowned in the brown Mersey,
disgorged on an evening tide,
nothing in her pocket, no note,
no clue to her identity :
the river released her at Wallasey.

Those words recorded by Virginia Woolf —
did they resound when, forty years later,
she herself waded into water,
placing the heavy stone in her pocket,
leaving her stick on the bank of the Ouse,
leaving her husband to mourn his release
from her madness, as the bombers,
hunting their targets, pulsed
over London, over the Serpentine,
dousing the light of moon and stars.

JANUARY 15th, 1991

Today a deadline looms —
the word now laden
with literal menace.
Afternoon sun lights the ice,
frost doesn't melt,
ponds have their protective cover.
But in Baghdad the heat intensifies;
people try to pretend
this day's like any other —
traffic on boulevards,
shoppers, workers, the fatalistic shrug;
kebab stalls rotate legs, shoulders
of lamb. Keep up routines.
Perhaps the worst will not happen.

Someone in Westminster throws
red powder-paint
over the Members of Parliament.

HEDGING

Hedges : traditional boundaries
protecting, enclosing —
keeping creatures in,
keeping creatures out.
Ambivalent in function,
like a yawn or a shout.
I'm told Spring is the season
for pleaching — the time for laying-in,
for chopping back the natural fence :
my neighbour says it's tidy —
country sense.
The hedge is *his,* he claims,
proved by the deeds. My trees —
beech, quickthorn, spindle —
lopped, with weeds, he's bonfired;
and branches, half-cut, about stakes
he's twined, as plashers packed in wedges —
so hedges become trees and trees hedges.

When challenged, he hedges,
smiles, bluffs it out,
neatly laying-in words
with thorns concealed.
His wife's pleased, too :
the view of hills revealed —
and the gardens of friends.
My privacy is destroyed, with nests,
my shade thinned out.
No doubt his craft's effective —
piracy. I'll bide my time
with seasons, flowers, bees,
planting tall saplings of willow, poplar, pine
on the side of the barrier that's mine —
so trees become hedges and hedges trees.

A TOWN IN OLD PHOTOGRAPHS

Not a guide book, yet essential
for my journey. A mapping of the past
which penetrates the present —
so many known places in period guise,
so many unknown people breathing
at the front of the century.

Some are walking under the park poplars
smaller by seventy years.
Looping Shrewsbury, an earlier Severn.
Whether the boating group on the quay
have just returned or are setting off,
I cannot decide. A school-capped boy
holds his mother's hand : he is forever
part of her skirt; the river's ripples
forever part of the wake
of a boat passed out of the picture.

A funeral procession possesses the road,
black-plumed horses pulling shiny carriages —
inside are the women mourners of D. O. Jones.
All the men are walking; one is waving
to someone not in the photograph,
the shadow of his arm a sundial on the wall.

In Butcher Row, street waifs have stopped playing.
A boy pulling faces at the camera
wears ragged clothes three sizes too large —
when grown into them, he will also be ripe
for a uniform, puttees, a gun.

At Hudson's Boat Yard, 'Coracles For Hire';
rowing boats are tethered; a gondola
glides, two blurred ghosts inside.

On a high building, the clock shows five exactly,
whether a.m. or p.m. is divulged by the empty street —
not one Edwardian person treads the damp cobbles.
Yet perhaps the clock's a deceit :
no sunlight to give a clue by angles,
no other clock as a check to the first.
Time, the tormentor.

ACROSS THE BERWYNS

Snowfall slither. A warning on the sign
at the bottom of the B road climb.
I'm seeking the ice plateau,
need, after fire, the salving
of snowscapes, white silence.

Higher now, the windscreen furred.
Pheasants flounder along the verge,
stunned by starvation
in stalactite copses.
Across the tops in frozen cloud —
heights, depths are lost,
Cadair Bronwen obliterated :
this mountain roof could be
the floor of a valley, the edge of fens.
Windscreen wipers carve an igloo door.
I stop, take small comforts —
coffee, chocolate, my pen;
like Scott, making nature notes which say
'I am here' . . . 'I was here' . . . 'today'.
Observations. Cwms are snowpools.
The wind trawls loose snow,
whirls new layers.
Somewhere down there Bala's sludge-brown streets,
bar snacks, provisions, takeaways.
Up here the white table offers no feast —
human and beast, we take our chance.
Water, yes — here are the blaenau,
but covert now, undiscoverable;
the only water flowing
slides inside rock or under ice.

The silence overflows.
I've reached for icicle coolness,
find that this, too, burns.